MOSES

AND THE YOKE OF FIRE

by

Wm. W. We

Independently published: Wm. W. Wells. Bacliff, Texas.

ISBN: 979-8-87165-384-5

PREFACE

Michaelangelo's wonderful marble statue of Moses, complete with hair protrusions, a subtle indication of horns, (his indication of strength, virility and wisdom), creates the image of a man set in stone for all of history. This Bible study will begin long before that. We begin with the man of flesh and blood, a flawed man who is called to his yoke of destiny by a fire in the desert, and is reshaped by his interactions with his Creator to become our God's spokesman and man of destiny.

Michaelangelo's tribute is fitting for the greatness of the man that God created through the burning yoke of fire placed upon this Moses in his wilderness exile. What a wonderful sight it would have been to have seen a desert nomad, trembling with fear and fire, step before the pharaoh to lay before him the demands of the Lord of all the universe. How did the highest of all the kings of this world at the time view this odd intrusion? Did curiosity open the chamber to the throne room, much like that of Jonah, bleached white and missing hair from time in the belly of a whale, a demented Gollum sent to warn the king of Nineveh? Moses shatters business as usual by challenging the man who decides life and death at his whim.

For forty years Moses will shoulder the burden of a grumbling and rebellious horde. Every time he turns to complain of the weight, God chisels off another sharp edge, until the man who stands atop Mount Pisgah to overlook the land of promise is the perfect representative of God to his people, one

4.   Moses and the Yoke of Fire

whom they will sorely miss, and remember forever. The tribute chisled in marble was forged in the desert under a yoke of fire.

TABLE OF CONTENTS

 Moses and the Yoke of Fire

CHAPTER 1:   INTRODUCTION

> As the sun was going down, a deep sleep fell on Abram. And behold, dreadful and great darkness fell upon him. Then the LORD said to Abram, "Know for certain that your offspring will be sojourners in a land that is not theirs and will be servants there, and they will be afflicted for four hundred years. But I will bring judgment on the nation that they serve, and afterward they shall come out with great possessions" (Gen. 15:12-14).

Destiny Foretold

The story of the Exodus begins hundreds of years before the birth of Moses. It begins with Abraham and his covenant with God. The reason for the flight from Egypt begins with the enigmatic passage above.

The quotation above begs for some explanation. This dark announcement of four hundred years of affliction could be nothing more than information, but, in context, it seems that Abraham may have failed in some way leading to a curse of four hundred years. Genesis 15 tells us that God appeared to

Abraham, (who is still referred to by his given name Abram at this point in the narrative), letting him know that his descendants will be as numerous as the sands by the seaside. He further instructs Abraham to prepare a sacrifice which will seal God's covenant with Abraham and his descendants.

Not only is Abraham to have countless descendants, but his descendants will receive the land, in which Abraham now dwells as a stranger. It will be their own. Having prepared the sacrifice, Abraham is made to wait. As darkness falls, he must chase scavenging birds from attacking the carcasses. Finally, he is overcome by sleepiness. In Abraham's defense, this is no natural sleepiness. The text says, "dreadful and great darkness fell upon him" (Gen. 15:12). This sounds to my ears as a spiritual attack of some sort, or it may simply be that God's appearance in the "smoking fire pot" (Gen. 15:17) was more than Abraham could handle. It is then that the curse is pronounced. But why? Your answer to this question will likely reflect how you understand the slavery of the children of Israel in Egypt, of which Abraham is immediately informed.

Levi and Simeon

Also bordering on a curse, there is one more bit of information that we must cover. This one applies to the lineage of Moses, Aaron and Miriam. For this, we skip ahead to Abraham's grandson Jacob, who has been given the name 'Israel' by God. Jacob now has twelve sons and a daughter. Genesis chapter 34 outlines a troubling story, and this one also leaves more questions than answers. Jacob's daughter Dinah is "humiliated" by Shechem, who is the son of Hamor, the ruler of the region in which Jacob and his family are living. This may have been a forcible rape, or it may have been a moment of indiscretion on the part of the two young people. In any case, Shechem is in love with Dinah and wants very much to have her as his wife.

Hamor and his son Shechem come to Jacob and his sons to ask for Dinah's hand in marriage and to offer to join together their communities through trade and marriage arrangements.

> Shechem also said to her father and to her brothers, "Let me find favor in your eyes, and whatever you say to me I will give. Ask me for as great a bride price and gift as you will, and I will give whatever you say to me. Only give me the young woman to be my wife."
>
> The sons of Jacob answered Shechem and his father Hamor deceitfully, because he had defiled their sister Dinah. They said to them, "We cannot do this thing, to give our sister to one who is uncircumcised, for that would be a disgrace to us. Only on this condition will we agree with you—that you will become as we are by every male among you being circumcised. Then we will give our daughters to you, and we will take your daughters to ourselves, and we will dwell with you and become one people. But if you will not listen to us and be circumcised, then we will take our daughter, and we will be gone" (Gen. 34:11-17).

Not suspecting foul play, Hamor and Shechem are delighted with the arrangement and agree to the terms established by the sons of Jacob. They then present the proposal to their community, arguing that the arrangement will benefit both communities. They then proceed to immediately circumcise all the men of the city. As we saw above, the sons of Jacob had answered deceitfully:

> On the third day, when they were sore, two of the sons of Jacob, Simeon and Levi, Dinah's brothers, took their swords and came against the city while it felt secure and killed all the males. They killed Hamor and his son Shechem with the sword and took Dinah out of Shechem's house and went away. The sons of Jacob came upon the slain and plundered the city, because they had defiled their sister (Gen. 34:25-27).

Levi's Legacy

Jacob is unhappy with his two sons who have willfully gone against his word of agreement with the men of Shechem:

> Then Jacob said to Simeon and Levi, "You have brought trouble on me by making me stink to the inhabitants of the land, the Canaanites and the Perizzites. My numbers are few, and if they gather themselves against me and attack me, I shall be destroyed, both I and my household." But they said, "Should he treat our sister like a prostitute?" (Gen. 34:30-31).

The legacy of this self-righteous act of violence hangs over the two brothers in perpetuity. Chapter 49 opens with an aged Jacob gathering his sons together, "that I may tell you what shall happen to you in days to come." While what follows is often regarded as Jacob blessing his sons, in the case of Levi and Simeon, blessing does not appear to be what is spoken over the two:

> "Simeon and Levi are brothers; weapons of violence are their swords. Let my soul come not into their council; O my glory, be not joined to their company. For in their anger they killed men, and in their willfulness they hamstrung oxen. Cursed be their anger, for it is fierce, and their wrath, for it is cruel! I will divide them in Jacob and scatter them in Israel" (Gen. 49:5-7).

Again, spinning forward many years, Moses is born a Levite who steps into history, not under the visible cloud of glorious destiny, but a man under a heavy burden. As a cruel four centuries of slavery nears its end, although no end is visible on the horizon, this child is born under the cloud of a generational curse of self-will and violence. More still, by the pharaoh's command, he and all Hebrew newborn male children are to be put to death immediately upon birth (Exo. 1:16).

A Man of Many Destinies

Michaelangelo's exquisite statue of Moses carved in marble leaves the impression of a man established by God for his place in history. But the biblical record seems to undermine the image set in stone. The world offered Moses more than one destiny. He was eighty years old, standing before a burning bush in the desert, before he reluctantly accepted God's chosen destiny for him. It was only the itch of the still small voice inside of him that caused him to step into the fire of a destiny written in grief, sorrow and ecstasy, and even at that, he insisted on a helper to share this yoke.

# 14.	Moses and the Yoke of Fire

This is in no way an attempt to diminish the nobility of Moses that is cherished by history. It is an attempt to reveal the flesh and blood person Moses, and so show that those of us who may be still be struggling to find our own God given place in the world have every reason to continue to hope for our own burning bush.

We live in a world of choices, paths to various destinies. Only God knows us well enough to point us to the true calling of heaven. In looking at the life of Moses, we will catch pointers on how to find God's highest calling designed specifically with you in mind.

Discussion Points:

1. What do you suppose was the reason for the children of Israel to suffer 400 years of slavery? Did Abraham fail in some way, or was it a necessary prerequisite to the blessings Israel was to receive?

2. We will see that the curse of his ancestor Levi causes Moses to have difficulties in life, so why do you think that God chose Moses to lead Israel?

3. The fifth commandment is to "Honor your father and your mother, that your days may be long in the land that the LORD your God is giving you" (Exo. 20:12), which Levi seems to have disregarded; so how does this command figure into Moses' destiny?

4. Is it possible that God was against Jacob's treaty with Shechem? In which case, were Levi and Simeon right to go against their father's wishes?

Application:

1. We are not all blessed to be born under a bright star, or with a silver spoon. Is our destiny fixed by God at birth, or do we choose our destiny?

2. Does in not appear that God makes odd choices when choosing a path of destiny for his saints? What sort of unexpected destiny might your future hold?

3. Honoring those who stand in authority over us, sometimes under difficult circumstance, seems important to God. How have you succeeded or failed in this regard?

4. Are there times when you have gone against a parent or authority, but, at the time, felt it was the right thing to do, despite the consequences?

CHAPTER 2:   THE BEAUTIFUL CHILD

> When she could hide him no longer,
> she took for him a basket made of
> bulrushes and daubed it with bitu-
> men and pitch. She put the child in it
> and placed it among the reeds by the
> river bank (Exo. 2:3).

Reading: **Exodus 2:1-22**

Born Under a Dark Star

My introduction doesn't introduce us to Moses, but rather to the legacy that he is born into. Moses himself is born in Egypt at the tail end of four centuries of bondage. He and his kin are slaves being cruelly treated by their Egyptian masters. More-over, he is born into the family line of Levi, thus, all of the things spoken over Levi and his offspring apply to Moses. In review, remember that Jacob pronounced over Levi and Sim-eon, "Cursed be their anger, for it is fierce, and their wrath, for it is cruel!" (Gen. 49:7). A curse, to an Israelite, was a serious thing. This beautiful child, or a "fine child" as the ESV renders it (Exo. 2:2), will struggle with self-righteous anger all of his life.

In the first chapter of the book of the Exodus, Pharaoh had ordered that all of the male newborns of the Hebrew women were to be killed (Exo. 1:16). When the Hebrew midwives failed to do as they were told, "the king gave a command to everyone in the nation, 'As soon as a Hebrew boy is born, throw him into the Nile River! But you can let the girls live'" (Exo 1:22). As a result, the birth of Moses was surrounded by anxiety and fear.

Moses is born to Amram and Jochebed (Exo. 6:20), both of the tribe of Levi. Moses was a "fine child", which is to say that he was a healthy child, and, for fear of Pharaoh's edict, he was kept hidden. After three months, it was no longer possible to keep him hidden, so his mother reluctantly takes a reed basket and covers it in pitch to make is water tight, and sets the basket, with Moses inside, in the river Nile. Moses has a brother Aaron, three years older (Exo. 7:7), born before Pharoah's latest edict, and a sister Miriam. It is assumed that Miriam was the eldest sibling as she is beside the river to watch over the basket (Exo. 2:4).

Drawn from the Water

The basket is spotted by the pharaoh's daughter, who has her attending maidens rescue Moses from the river. Emerging out of the nearby bushes, Miriam offers to find a nursemaid for the child (Exo. 2:5-7). Ironically, Moses' actual mother becomes the hired nursemaid on behalf of Pharaoh's daughter who adopts him (Exo. 2:8-9). Thus, the child, meant for instant death, is instead raised as a prince of Egypt, a stark turn of events.

> When the child grew older, she brought him to Pharaoh's daughter, and he became her son. She named him Moses, "Because,"

she said, "I drew him out of the water"
(Exo. 2:10).

In Egyptian, the name "Moses" means "son". In Hebrew, the name means "drawn out, or rescued," thus out of the water. I assume that Pharaoh's daughter is the one doing the naming, so this could be a Hebrew coloration established by history, or possibly Miriam suggested the name. The latter suggestion seems less likely given the animosity of the Egyptians, Pharaoh in particular, towards the Hebrews at the time.

While the Egyptians left a considerable history of the various pharaohs and their wives, the exact timing of the events of this chapter are hotly debated. The most commonly suggested name for the pharaoh at the time of the Exodus is that of Ramesses II (c. 1279–1213 BC). Exo. 1:11 says that The Hebrew slaves were building the store city of "Raamses" (Exo. 1:11). Ramesses' father Seti I would then be the pharaoh who ordered the death of the Hebrew children. One of Ramesses' two sisters Tia and Henutmire, (the latter becoming one of Ramesses II eight royal wives as well), would be the one who rescued and raised Moses.

Four hundred years prior to the reign of Ramesses II, the Hyksos, a semitic tribe, ruled Egypt. Thus, Joseph would not have seemed strange as an Egyptian ruler. When the Hyksos rulers were driven from the throne in approximately 1530 BC, the semitic presence suddenly became loathsome, (the Hyksos were not particularly benevolent rulers), hence the slavery of semitic tribes.

Was Moses Groomed for Power?

One of the more intriguing suggestions is that the daughter who raised Moses was Hatshepsut, daughter of Thutmose I. She married her half-brother Thutmose II, (a common practice within the royal houses of Egypt), but had no children. On the death of Thutmose II, her stepson Thutmose III was only two, so she ruled as regent for six years until she made herself a pharaoh (c. 1473–1458 BC) alongside of him. While the timeline for this suggestion would put Joseph prior to Hyksos rule, making her a less probable candidate for Moses' foster mom, it does suggest the possibility that Moses was being groomed to serve as a royal son, and thus a potential pharaoh, should an accident happen to Thutmose III. Such "accidents" were not infrequent in Egypt.

There are other possibilities, each with their own intriguing story line, but we really don't know who the pharaoh was at the time of Moses. I only mention all of this to point out that the adoption of Moses into the royal family could have had serious political meaning. For Moses, the difference was night and day. He went from a destiny of early death, to the destiny of political significance in the most powerful kingdom of its day. At the same time, it appears that Moses was well aware of where he came from. It is not unlikely that his Egyptian foster mother knew that the wet nurse was his biological mother. We will see that Moses knows that he has a Hebrew brother and sister before he returns to Egypt. The young man Moses was a man with a foot in two worlds, or perhaps it would be better to suggest that he had both feet in the world of the Egyptian court of the pharaoh, but a toe-hold of wonder about his Hebrew ancestry.

A Fateful Blow

And so, "One day, when Moses had grown up, he went out to his people and looked on their burdens" (Exo. 2:11). Something inside of the man turned him away from the halls of political power, with all of its pomp and nasty intrigues, to his own people, a people that he barely knew. On seeing one of the Hebrew slaves being beaten without mercy by an Egyptian, an indignation rose up in him. His sense of justice was deeply offended. "He looked this way and that, and seeing no one, he struck down the Egyptian and hid him in the sand" (Exo. 2:12). His legacy as one of the sons of Levi had boiled to the surface; self-righteous anger took the life of an Egyptian in defense of a Hebrew slave.

Although Moses still made his bed in Pharaoh's palace, he had just made a choice to uphold the rights of the underdog Hebrews against those of the Egyptian overlords. Moses no longer identified as an Egyptian. His adoptive home was no longer where his heart resided.

It did not take long for the consequences of his actions to surface. In fact, according to the account, the next day he tries to stop a fight between two Hebrews, only to have one challenge him, "Who made you a prince and a judge over us? Do you mean to kill me as you killed the Egyptian?" (Exo. 2:14). Immediately, Moses realizes that he is in deep trouble, the deed is known. Siding with the underdog against Pharaoh's men had very deadly consequences which he well knew.

"When Pharaoh heard of it, he sought to kill Moses. But Moses fled from Pharaoh and stayed in the land of Midian" (Exo. 2:15). The die is cast, Moses is now a fugitive from Pharaoh's palace, and from the people of the brick kilns that he had thought to protect. And so begins forty years of exile.

Moses joins the family of Reuel, priest of Midian (Exo. 2:16, 21). The Midianite tribe descended from Abraham through Ketura, his wife after the death of Sarah (Gen. 25:1-2). This makes Reuel a distant relative, but not part of the covenant of Israel. Moses marries Zipporah, one of Reuel's seven daughters, and settles down to a very different life, the life of a shepherd in the desert of Midian, far from the green banks of the river Nile.

Discussion Points:

1. The birth of a boy into Amram's household must have had a wide range of competing emotions. Considering Pharaoh's edict, how do you suppose the family felt?

2. What do you suppose drove Pharaoh's daughter to rescue a Hebrew child condemned to death by her father?

3. Moses seemed to have had a bright future in the world of the Egyptian palace, what made him choose to set his heart on his natural kin?

4. By murdering an Egyptian, Moses was forced to flee both the palace and the brick kilns. How do you suppose he felt as he left Egypt behind?

Application:

1. How do you suppose your family felt when you were born? Compare that with the circumstances Moses was born into.

2. Have you been helped or hurt in life by circumstances that didn't seem logical at the time, and maybe still doesn't seem logical?

3. Have you ever had to choose to leave behind a potentially bright future, for an uncertain future that seemed to be more "right"?

4. Have you ever been in a position of leaving your life situation behind, but wishing you had a better choice in the matter?

CHAPTER 3:   A BURNING BUSH

And the angel of the LORD appeared to him in a flame of fire out of the midst of a bush. He looked, and behold, the bush was burning, yet it was not consumed. And Moses said, "I will turn aside to see this great sight, why the bush is not burned." When the LORD saw that he turned aside to see, God called to him out of the bush, "Moses, Moses!" And he said, "Here I am" (Exo. 3:2-4).

Reading: **Exodus 3:1 thru 4:17**

The Shepherd

Both Moses and David were shepherds before they were called into leadership roles. In fact, Abraham, Isaac and Jacob were shepherds all. Israel was a nation of shepherds. The character trait most commonly associated with the shepherd is that of care. The shepherd must make sure the flock is watered and fed. The shepherd pays attention for various signs of disease that might attack the flock. The shepherd watches for predators lurking in the darkness, and because of those predators, the shepherd watches to make sure that none of the sheep wander off where they are alone and unprotected.

There is something else worth considering. The shepherd spends a lot of time alone with the flock. The shepherd has time to think, to meditate, and to talk to God. It is not surprising, therefore, that Jesus makes frequent reference to shepherds and shepherding as he describes his ministry and therefore the ministry of the body of Christ.

Isn't it interesting that the man who had grown up in the halls of power politics is forced to flee into the desert to become a shepherd. By tradition, Moses was forty years old when he fled into the desert, as noted by Stephen in his defense (Acts 7:22-24), and he spent another forty years in the wilderness before he could return to lead Israel out of Egypt (Acts 7:30). Having learned all of the devices of the politically powerful, Moses is sent to learn what it takes to be a person who cares, who nurtures and stands guard to protect.

At the end of this training period, Moses is no longer the impulsive fire breathing "savior". In fact, he doubts whether he is able to take on the task that God is about to lay upon him.

I Will Turn Aside to See

Surrounded by sheep in the midst of a rugged and barren wasteland, Moses looks up to see a bush, seemingly on fire, but the bush is not consumed (Exo. 3:2). And so, he turns aside, that is, he goes out of his way to approach the burning bush (Exo. 3:3). It seems that there was some significance to Moses turning aside to look, for, "When the LORD saw that he turned aside to see, God called to him out of the bush, 'Moses, Moses!' And he said, 'Here I am'" (Exo. 3:4). It is as if he is being drawn as a moth to a flame. But this flame is no earthly flame. Is it possible that if he had not been ready, Moses would have been repelled by this flame?

God begins to speak to Moses. Moses does not appear to be shocked that God is here, although this manifest presence is terrifying, and he clearly believes that if he sees God he could die on the spot (Exo. 3:6). Like David, Moses seems to have developed a relationship with God, we could call it an intuitive relationship; he knows God's presence, but not His manifestation. This is new.

God stops Moses and tells him to remove his sandals before approaching (Exo. 3:5). This is a theme we will explore in future chapters: when the presence of God is powerful, as it is in this instance, it is important to stay attentive and respectful. He removes his sandals as a sign of respect.

God gets right down to business. He has a plan to deliver the people of Israel out of the tyranny of Pharaoh, and He wants Moses to be a major part of this plan:

> "And now, behold, the cry of the people of Israel has come to me, and I have also seen the oppression with which the Egyptians oppress them. Come, I will send you to Pharaoh that you may bring my people, the children of Israel, out of Egypt" (Exo. 3:9-10).

Forty years previously, Moses was gung-ho and headstrong; a child of palace politics, he was ready to dispense justice and take the reins of power. After forty years as a shepherd, he is quick to distrust his own self-assurance. His desert flock was not what he was raised to imagine he'd be leading, but it had taught him to be wary of his own judgements. And so, Moses answers, "Who am I that I should go to Pharaoh and bring the children of Israel out of Egypt?" (Exo. 3:11).

Negotiations

God assures the reluctant Moses:

> "But I will be with you, and this shall be the sign for you, that I have sent you: when you have brought the people out of Egypt, you shall serve God on this mountain" (Exo. 3:12).

It is not totally clear whether the sign mentioned is that God will be with Moses, or that the sign will be that Moses will accomplish the task and bring Israel to this mountain to worship. Most translations seem to hedge towards the latter understanding.

Moses is thinking about this. Thinking causes him to begin to hesitate, to see problems, and throw up multiple what ifs. He is well aware that the Hebrews have adopted all sorts of household gods from Egypt and from the many other cultures that they have been rubbing shoulders with. But Abraham's god is "the God." Moses is trying to imagine how he is to present this one God to a people with many gods. He asks God, what name he should give them to distinguish this God. The response is a riddle: "God said to Moses, 'I AM WHO I AM.' And he said, 'Say this to the people of Israel, "I AM has sent me to you"'" (Exo. 3:14).

God is saying that He is beyond worldly names, He cannot be compared with any other god. He IS and the I AM has a plan. God then briefly outlines His plan to send Moses to the elders of Israel and then to Pharaoh. God knows that Pharaoh will resist and have to be forced to let Israel go by miraculous signs and wonders, but when they do go, they will be thrust out with lavish gifts (Exo. 3:15-22).

Notice that God has just outlined what is about to happen. Unfortunately, Moses is busy thinking this through. He sees all sorts of problems with God's plan. To start with, Moses is sure that the elders of Israel "will not believe me or listen to my voice" (Exo. 4:1). God describes three miracles that Moses will be able to perform to convince the reluctant elders.

This is not the end of Moses' issues with God's plan: "Oh, my Lord, I am not eloquent, either in the past or since you have spoken to your servant, but I am slow of speech and of tongue" (4:10). Was this true? We don't know. It may be that after so many years as a shepherd, he simply distrusted his ability to speak in the latest fashion of an Egyptian statesman. In any case, God is having none of it. He insists that He will be there to give Moses the right words to speak. But, Moses resists, "Oh, my Lord, please send someone else" (Exo. 4:13).

> Then the anger of the LORD was kindled against Moses and he said, "Is there not Aaron, your brother, the Levite? I know that he can speak well. Behold, he is coming out to meet you, and when he sees you, he will be glad in his heart. You shall speak to him and put the words in his mouth, and I will be with your mouth and with his mouth and will teach you both what to do. He shall speak for you to the people, and he shall be your mouth, and you shall be as God to him. And take in your hand this staff, with which you shall do the signs" (Exo. 4:14-17).

Aaron is already on his way to Moses; we assume that God has sent him. We can see from the exchange, however, that having Aaron be a substitute spokesman is not God's desire.

Discussion Points:

1. In your own words, how do you think that Moses' time of shepherding effected his call to lead?

2. What do suppose the significance of "turning aside to see" is? What do you suppose Moses' relationship to God was prior to the burning bush incident?

3. Moses has clearly developed a relationship with God during his stay in Midian. Why do you think that he is so hesitant to do as God is asking him?

4. God says to Moses, tell them "I AM has sent me to you." What sort of message is being conveyed in this cryptic name?

Application:

1. How would you rate your own shepherding or caring skills? Short of becoming a shepherd for forty years, are there ways you might improve?

2. Have you experienced spiritual manifestations, godly or otherwise? Did they draw you in, or repel you?

3. Have you ever hesitated to do something that you had a feeling that God wanted you to do?

4. When you pray, where do you direct your prayers? Do you have a specific image of God?

CHAPTER 4:   FAMILY ISSUES

Then Zipporah took a flint and cut off her son's foreskin and touched Moses' feet with it and said, "Surely you are a bridegroom of blood to me!" (Exo. 4:25).

Reading: **Exodus 4:18-31 and 18:1-27**

Numbers 12:1-18

Zipporah

We like to think that a man of such spiritual stature would have a loving and supportive family life. This does not appear to have been the case with Moses. Scripture does not give us very much to go on, but what we do have looks ominous.

There is no indication of trouble until Moses packs up the wife and kids to return to Egypt. Scripture simply says, "At a lodging place on the way the LORD met him and sought to put him to death" (Exo. 4:24). There is no indication of what that looked like, but we might assume that Moses fell violently ill. What is interesting is that his wife Zipporah seems to know immediately that this is from God, *and why*.

Zipporah circumcises their sons. "So he let him alone. It was then that she said, 'A bridegroom of blood,' because of the circumcision" (Exo. 4:26). I have to assume that Zipporah and Moses have been quarreling over this issue. As Midianites, and therefore descendants of Abraham, one would have thought that Zipporah and her father, the priest of Midian, would have been familiar with circumcision. It is possible that a circumcision had gone badly sometime in the family line, so that Zipporah feared it. We just don't know. Clearly, Zipporah knew what to do, and, moreover, she understood why it had to be done. But she wasn't happy about it.

After this, we don't hear anything about Zipporah and the two boys until much later, after Moses and all of Israel have taken leave of Egypt, left Pharaoh's army drowned in the Red Sea, and arrived at the mountain of God.

> Jethro, the priest of Midian, Moses' father-in-law, heard of all that God had done for Moses and for Israel his people, how the LORD had brought Israel out of Egypt.
>
> Now Jethro, Moses' father-in-law, had taken Zipporah, Moses' wife, after he had sent her home, along with her two sons. The name of the one was Gershom (for he said, "I have been a sojourner in a foreign land"), and the name of the other, Eliezer (for he said, "The God of my father was my help, and delivered me from the sword of Pharaoh"). Jethro, Moses' father-in-law, came with his sons and his wife to Moses in the wilderness where he was encamped at the mountain of God (Exo. 18:1-5).

We don't know when or why Zipporah took the boys and returned home. All we have to go on is this mention that Jethro brought them with him when he came to meet Moses, after they had been sent home.

Jethro

Introduced as Moses' father-in-law, it is more likely that Jethro was Moses' brother-in-law, or an uncle to Zipporah. Apparently, the word in Hebrew simply means a male relative by marriage, and we were first introduced to Reuel as the father of Zipporah and her sisters. It makes sense that Reuel has died by the time of Moses' return to Egypt forty years later, and so Jethro is now the priest of Midian and patriarch of Zipporah's clan. Thus, Moses asks permission to return to Egypt from Jethro (Exo. 4:18).

Later, we will be introduced to Hobab who is introduced as "the son of Reuel the Midianite, Moses' father-in-law" (Num. 10:29). Also, a brother-in-law, Moses asks Hobab to travel with Israel as a guide through the wastelands, which we assume he does, as his descendants appear among the Israelites in the book of Judges (Judg. 4:11). Jethro, who is now the priest of Midian and likely the patriarch of the tribe, would have had to return to Midian to resume the care for his clan (Exo. 18:27).

As we saw, when Moses brings the children of Israel to the mountain of God, Jethro brings Zipporah and the children to him (Exo. 18:5). Whether Zipporah stays with Moses and Israel or returns to Midian is not clear, but Gershom and Eliezer's descendants do appear in the chronology of Israel (Judg. 18:30; 1 Chron. 26:24-25), so we must assume that his boys stay with him this time.

Jethro is a positive figure here. Where Zipporah appears to be a reluctant bride, Jethro is impressed with all that Moses has accomplished: "Blessed be the LORD, who has delivered you out of the hand of the Egyptians and out of the hand of Pharaoh and has delivered the people from under the hand of the Egyptians. Now I know that the LORD is greater than all gods, because in this affair they dealt arrogantly with the people" (Exo. 18:10-11). As a leader and priest of Midian, Jethro offers a sacrifice and hosts a meal for the elders of Israel, a gesture of diplomatic welcome (Exo. 18:12).

On the following day, Jethro observes Moses handling issues among the thousands of complainants that appear before him, Jethro pulls him aside to advise him to delegate authority so as to lessen the burden on his shoulders (Exo. 18:14-24). With a leadership role in Midian, Jethro is perfectly positioned to give Moses wise counsel in this matter. He is a friendly and helpful figure.

Gershom and Eliezer

It is curious that Moses' two sons play no significant role in Israel during their father's lifetime. They are listed as Levites in the later annuls of Israel. Because their mother was a Midianite, and thus not of the covenant of Israel, this may be the reason for their disqualification from the priesthood, which falls to Aaron and his sons. Gershom's descendants do appear as officers in charge of the treasury under David (1 Chron. 26:24).

It is also possible that Zipporah's presumed difficult relationship with Moses transferred to the two boys as well, making them unhelpful in managing the tribes of Israel. Scripture gives us no direction in these cases, but the questions raised are interesting, even if answers remain speculative at best. What these questions strike at is the unreliability of portions of Moses' support system.

Aaron and Miriam

Unreliable support doesn't fully cover Moses' siblings. The book of Numbers chapter 12 begins: "Miriam and Aaron spoke against Moses because of the Cushite woman whom he had married, for he had married a Cushite woman." Cush is usually assumed have referred to the African kingdom just south of Egypt, what is now Sudan.[1] Zipporah, we have to assume, was Midianite, so this might suggest that Zipporah left with Jethro and returned to Midian or that she has died. Moses has taken a new wife, a Cushite.

It should be noted that when the children of Israel went out from Egypt, "A mixed multitude also went up with them" (Exo. 12:38). Mosaic law has several ordinances governing the treatment of "strangers" amongst Israel, those who would serve their same God (as: Exo. 12:48). So, the presence of a Cushite, a black African, was perfectly reasonable. It appears that Moses had taken one as his second wife. It is unlikely that Miriam and Aaron's quarrel was racial, but the fact that this woman was of a different culture from the Semitic tribes of Abraham, i.e., she was an outsider, upset them, giving them reason for rebellion. Unfortunately, we know nothing more than this about this woman.

---

[1] Some place Cush in what is now Yemen, which was the part of Arabia with extensive trading ties with Africa.

By this time, Moses has spent countless hours in direct communication with God Himself. Opposing Moses was a bad idea. God intervenes immediately, making it abundantly clear that Moses is special:

> "Hear my words: If there is a prophet among you, I the LORD make myself known to him in a vision; I speak with him in a dream. Not so with my servant Moses. He is faithful in all my house. With him I speak mouth to mouth, clearly, and not in riddles, and he beholds the form of the LORD. Why then were you not afraid to speak against my servant Moses?" (Num 12:6-8).

The cloud of God's presence departs immediately, leaving Miriam, who was undoubted the instigator, leprous. Despite the rebellion, Moses intercedes for Miriam. God returns to add, "If her father had but spit in her face, should she not be shamed seven days? Let her be shut outside the camp seven days, and after that she may be brought in again" (Num. 12:14).

In keeping with his humble posture, developed, no doubt, by his close contact with God, it is very likely that Moses stayed tight lipped about this incident. His cousins, unaware of how quickly God will react to defend Moses, will soon attempt an even more forceful rebellion, with a much greater harm to themselves (Num. 16:1-50).

But first, in the next chapter, we should return to Moses as he arrives in Egypt to confront Pharoah.

Discussion Points:

1. It would appear that Moses does not have a reliable support system within his family. Would this have made his time with God even more important?

2. Jethro is one of the most, if not the most, important figure for his large tribe. How important do you suppose his faith and friendship was for Moses?

3. At a time in Israel's history when God seemed to be closing off Israel from outside influences, what do you suppose is the significance of Moses taking a foreign wife?

4. How significant do you think Miriam and Aaron's rebellion was for Moses personally? Do you suppose that Moses struggled with a strong sense of rejection? Discuss how God's quick response helps change the atmosphere.

Application:

1. You may or may not have good support within your family. Does that weaken or strengthen your reliance on God?

2. Are there people in your circle of friends and relations who are particularly important for giving you reassurance in times of stress?

3. Are your outside influences helping you or harming you? Usually, the answer is both. Discuss.

4. Do you struggle with feelings of a lack of support? Have you ever had to face significant opposition? Was there any backup there to support you at that time?

CHAPTER 5:   CONFRONTING PHARAOH

Then you shall say to Pharaoh, "Thus says the LORD, 'Israel is my firstborn son, and I say to you, "Let my son go that he may serve me." If you refuse to let him go, behold, I will kill your firstborn son'" (Exo. 4:22-23).

Reading: **Exodus 5:1 thru 6:13 and 7:1**

The Answer is No!

Moses had already been warned by God that Pharaoh will not cooperate, and that force will be necessary. The necessary force is not something that Moses can provide, and so he must believe that God will back up his every threat made in the great halls of power.

Notice that the beginning is cautious:

> Afterward Moses and Aaron went and said to Pharaoh, "Thus says the LORD, the God of Israel, 'Let my people go, that they may hold a feast to me in the wilderness'" (Exo. 5:1).

Using Aaron as his mouthpiece, Moses asks for permission to take his people into the wilderness to worship God. This is directed at a man who believes himself to be a god, so the answer is abrupt, "Who is the LORD, that I should obey his voice and let Israel go? I do not know the LORD, and moreover, I will not let Israel go" (Exo. 5:2).

To back up the power of his lordship, Pharaoh orders that the Israelites will no longer receive straw, but must gather the straw to make bricks, while still continuing to produce bricks at the same rate as before (Exo. 5:6-8). When the work falters due to the onerous requirements, the work bosses are called before Pharaoh for a dressing down. Emerging from their unhappy meeting, the work bosses find Moses and Aaron are waiting. Not surprisingly, the two receive an earful from these men. "The LORD look on you and judge, because you have made us stink in the sight of Pharaoh and his servants, and have put a sword in their hand to kill us" (Exo. 5:21).

He was already warned that the process is not going to be easy, yet Moses was clearly not ready for his own people turning against him. He takes the issue directly to God, "O Lord, why have you done evil to this people? Why did you ever send me? For since I came to Pharaoh to speak in your name, he has done evil to this people, and you have not delivered your people at all" (Exo. 5:22-23). He doesn't realize that he has barely dipped his toe in the water. This is going to be a long and difficult struggle. Complaining won't shorten the journey.

The Shepherd and the Cobra King

"See, I have made you like God to Pharaoh, and your brother Aaron shall be your prophet" (Exo. 7:1). Moses is being sent back to the pharaoh, but God outlines the difficult process to come in greater detail:

> "I will harden Pharaoh's heart, and though
> I multiply my signs and wonders in the land
> of Egypt, Pharaoh will not listen to you.
> Then I will lay my hand on Egypt and bring
> my hosts, my people the children of Israel,
> out of the land of Egypt by great acts of
> judgment" (Exo 7:3-4).

Moses and Aaron must return to the halls of power with the same request that has already irritated Pharaoh. This time they will be challenged to prove themselves. Aaron is holding the shepherd's rod from Moses' desert sojourn, which he casts before Pharaoh. It immediately turns into a serpent (Exo. 7:10). It should be noted that the serpent, specifically a cobra with hood flared, is the royal emblem worn on the foreheads of every pharaoh. Moses has called Pharaoh's challenge and returned the challenge by directly challenging his symbol and therefore his authority itself.

Pharaoh must answer the challenge. He immediately calls for his magicians, who also throw down their staffs and have them turn into serpents, but the shepherd's serpent swallows all the other serpents (Exo. 7:11-12). The most powerful ruler in the world at the time has been confronted, and the leader of the slaves has returned the challenge double using the most provocative symbol imaginable. The cobra king has been put on notice. "Still Pharaoh's heart was hardened, and he would not listen to them, as the LORD had said" (Exo. 7:13).

Fire from the Desert

At this point, God instructs Moses and Aaron to bring plagues upon Egypt, since Pharaoh refuses to submit to the request to allow the people to go out to serve the Lord in the desert. For this study, I will not be breaking down all the various plagues, which have often been associated with various gods of the Egyptians. This does not help us to understand Moses. What is of interest is that Moses appears to gain confidence as the plagues progress. Aaron strikes the Nile with the shepherd's rod to turn the river to blood (Exo. 7:19-20), again he uses the rod to cause frogs to come up on the land (Exo. 8:6), and again he strikes the ground causing swarms of gnats (Exo. 8:17). The swarm of flies appear without Aaron wielding the rod at all (Exo. 8:20-24). Alongside this something else is happening in this process, increasingly Moses seems to be speaking directly to Pharaoh, without Aaron intervening (Exo. 8:9-11 & 26-29). The narrative of the fifth plague doesn't even mention Aaron (Exo. 9:1-7).

Originally, Aaron was inserted as a crutch to bolster Moses' confidence. But seemingly Moses is less and less dependent on Aaron. It is Moses who throws dust in the air to initiate the plague of boils (Exo. 9:10), and again, it is Moses who stretches the shepherd's rod to heaven drawing down the hail (9:23), and again for the plague of locusts (Exo. 10:13) and the unnatural darkness (Exo. 10:22). Finally, Pharaoh, whose authority has withered plague by plague, exclaims "Get away from me; take care never to see my face again, for on the day you see my face you shall die" (Exo. 10:28). Moses' himself replies, and it is not the reply of someone intimidated by the serpent throne, "As you say! I will not see your face again" (Exo. 10:29).

Moses is now fully in charge. This is the preparation for the final plague, the death of all the first-born of Egypt. God instructs Moses to tell the Israelites to ask for gold and silver jewelry from their Egyptian neighbors. "And the LORD gave the people favor in the sight of the Egyptians. Moreover, the man Moses was very great in the land of Egypt, in the sight of Pharaoh's servants and in the sight of the people" (Exo. 11:3). At the end of chapter eleven, Moses stands before the servants of Pharaoh to deliver Pharaoh the news, all of your nations first-born will die. "And all these your servants shall come down to me and bow down to me, saying, 'Get out, you and all the people who follow you.' And after that I will go out." The text adds, "And he went out from Pharaoh in hot anger" (Exo. 11:8).

The meek shepherd, unwilling to return to Egypt without some sort of spokesman to stand between himself and the throne, is definitely gone. Moses is fully trusting in God's Word to him, and delivers it without the slightest hesitation. On top of that, he is filled with anger. Is this the anger of God that he senses, or is this the anger of centuries of injustice poured out against his people?

The final plague, the death of all the first-born of Egypt and the Passover of Israel was an act of God without intervention from Moses or Aaron other than their instructing the Israelites on how to cause the plague to pass over their own homes (Exo. 11:1 thru 12:32).

Discussion Points:

1. Pharaoh's "no," and the increased hardship on Israel has Moses running to God in complaint. Why does it seem that Moses is unsure of his footing with God?

2. The serpent being symbolic of the authority of the Egyptian Pharaoh, why do you suppose God chose a serpent for His first miraculous sign?

3. Seeing God at work in miraculous ways, Moses gains greater and greater confidence. What is giving Moses this confidence?

4. Discuss how this may have changed Aaron's role at his side?

Application:

1. Does it seem that your life's trajectory has been pointing you towards some specific role in God's Kingdom?

2. Sometimes we seem to run up against a brick wall at full speed, thinking God is with us. How do you deal with these setbacks?

3. Sometimes God does things to make a symbolic statement. Can you think of an instance in your own life where this may have occurred?

4. Have you seen God at work in your personal life? Does this give you greater confidence as you are called on to step out in faith?

48.   Moses and the Yoke of Fire

CHAPTER 6:   EXODUS

> Tell the people of Israel to turn back
> and encamp in front of Pi-hahiroth,
> between Migdol and the sea, in front
> of Baal-zephon; you shall encamp
> facing it, by the sea (Exo. 14:2).

Reading: **Exodus 14:1 thru 15:21**

A Test of Faith

All Israel and many who had joined themselves to the tribes of Israel are thrust out of Egypt carrying away a portion of the wealth of the land. Arrived at the edge of the wilderness (Exo. 13:20), God tells Moses to turn and camp in the sight of Egypt (Exo. 14:2), instead of fleeing beyond the reach of Egypt as fast as possible. God further tells Moses that He will harden Pharaoh's heart so that he will pursue them. God is not done showing His absolute power over Egypt and their king (Exo. 14:3).

Moses has come to trust that God will do as He says that He will do, and so he turns his company and camps in front of Pi-hahiroth, as God had instructed him to do. We really don't know exactly where this was. Many ideas circulate, but the most important point is that Egypt's army knew exactly where to find the fleeing slaves. This massive camp of poorly armed civilians raises their eyes to see that world's foremost army appear in the distance. Pharaoh, with six hundred of his elite chariots, and the Egyptian army with many more horsemen and chariots are on the horizon, and their intentions are most obviously murderous. All of the doubts and misgivings of the children of Israel bubble to the surface in an instant:

> "Is it because there are no graves in Egypt that you have taken us away to die in the wilderness? What have you done to us in bringing us out of Egypt? Is not this what we said to you in Egypt: 'Leave us alone that we may serve the Egyptians'? For it would have been better for us to serve the Egyptians than to die in the wilderness" (Exo. 14:11-12).

While the faith of his followers is badly shaken, Moses seems remarkably composed, telling them:

> "Fear not, stand firm, and see the salvation of the LORD, which he will work for you today. For the Egyptians whom you see today, you shall never see again. The LORD will fight for you, and you have only to be silent" (Exo. 14:13-14).

It should be noted that Moses has no idea how God is going to save them, but he expresses confidence that God has a plan up His sleeve, at least as he is speaking to the people. Moses is required to have enough faith to bring calm to a people who are concerned that their luck is about to run out. Moses knows that they aren't there by luck. The nation's fear weighs heavy on him. God sees nervousness and indecision in his heart:

> The LORD said to Moses, "Why do you cry to me? Tell the people of Israel to go

> forward. Lift up your staff, and stretch out
> your hand over the sea and divide it, that
> the people of Israel may go through the sea
> on dry ground" (Exo. 14:15-16).

While all of the miracles that have happened so far, could seemingly have naturalistic explanations, (and I have seen several such explanations), "go forward" and "stretch out your hand over the sea and divide it" is especially difficult to believe. But notice something else here, God says, "Why do you cry to me? Tell the people of Israel to go forward." Has God just told Moses not to ask for directions, but to divide the sea?

Baptism in Water

It seems that, Moses has just been given permission to declare a miracle to happen, and God will make it happen. In this case, He even suggests what Moses should declare. While the pillar of fire by night and cloud by day moves to block Pharaoh's army, Moses stretches out his hand, raising the shepherd's rod over the sea (Exo. 14:19-21).

At sunrise the next morning, the path of escape is laid before them; there is a path in the midst of the sea. "And the people of Israel went into the midst of the sea on dry ground, the waters being a wall to them on their right hand and on their left" (Exo. 14:22). Two million people must step down into the sea, while nothing but the invisible finger of God holds back the waters on both sides. At any moment those waters could be released and come crashing back into place. This is truly a crossing of faith, a water baptism intended to seal this multitude heart and soul to God.

When the pillar of fire and cloud lifts to allow the pursuing Egyptians to follow, they too enter between the walls of water. Unwilling to admit that the shepherd has beaten them, the might of Egypt steps into the miraculous opening. Now, the pillar of fire and cloud descends upon the arrogant army, throwing them into confusion, but when they turn to flee, God instructs Moses, "Stretch out your hand over the sea, that the water may come back upon the Egyptians, upon their chariots, and upon their horsemen" (Exo. 14:26).

A nervous band of civilians turn to see the pride of Egypt swallowed by the sea. They had just passed through the same sea unharmed, but now they watch as the bodies of Egyptian soldiers begin to wash ashore.

Praise God for Deliverance

This is the defining moment for Israel. When the people turn to see their former tormentors swallowed by the same sea that God has led them through unharmed. They now know that they have been set completely free, separated unto the God of Abraham, Isaac and Jacob. The children of Israel are now the nation of Israel, albeit still a nation still without a home. While there will be time to contemplate the process of seizing the land promised to them so long ago, now is the time to celebrate the weight of Egypt's yoke of bondage lifted and broken before them.

Moses leads them in praise, "The LORD is my strength and my song, and he has become my salvation; this is my God, and I will praise him, my father's God, and I will exalt him" (Exo. 15:2). Moses goes on:

"The peoples have heard; they tremble; pangs have seized the inhabitants of Philistia. Now are the chiefs of Edom dismayed; trembling seizes the leaders of Moab; all the inhabitants of Canaan have melted away. Terror and dread fall upon them; because of the greatness of your arm, they are still as a stone, till your people, O LORD, pass by, till the people pass by whom you have purchased.

"You will bring them in and plant them on your own mountain, the place, O LORD, which you have made for your abode, the sanctuary, O Lord, which your hands have established" (Exo. 15:14-17).

As you can see, the song of Moses not only praises God for what He has done in breaking the yoke of Egypt off the neck of Israel, but Moses reminds Israel that God intends to protect them and guide them into a land of their own and a faith of their own when He "plants them" on the mountain of God.

Discussion Points:

1. Moses has come to have a firm faith in God. He has become like God to his people. Israel has a shaky faith in God and Moses. Discuss how Moses handles their challenge at Pi-hahiroth facing baptism of faith at the Red Sea.

2. God says, "Why do you cry to me?" Is it possible that Moses is being given creative license to declare the miraculous on God's behalf? Does this imply that God has placed His trust in Moses?

3. With great relief, Israel turns to see the pursuing army destroyed. As they shout in praise and triumph, Moses reminds them there is still a road ahead that must be traveled. How does he sow hope and courage for the difficult road ahead?

4. What does it mean that God will "plant them" on the mountain of God?

Application:

1. Have you ever faced a challenge to your confidence
    that gave you pause? Has this ever been a situation
    where others health or well-being were at stake as
    well?

2. Some baptisms of faith are easy, but some are quite
    difficult. Can you discuss a difficult challenge that
    had to be gone through with in faith? How did it work
    out?

3. Have you been able to use past triumphs to bring
    hope and courage for future challenges? Have you
    any personal examples of God's help that can help
    you in future difficulties?

4. Do you feel "planted in God?" How would you de-
    scribe what that means to you?

56.   Moses and the Yoke of Fire

CHAPTER 7:   BREAD FROM HEAVEN

And the whole congregation of the people of Israel grumbled against Moses and Aaron in the wilderness, and the people of Israel said to them, "Would that we had died by the hand of the LORD in the land of Egypt, when we sat by the meat pots and ate bread to the full, for you have brought us out into this wilderness to kill this whole assembly with hunger." (Exo. 16:2-3).

Reading: **Exodus 16:1-36**

and Numbers 11:31-35

The Meat Pots of Yesterday

Moses, who has been in conversation with God during each leg of their journey so far, has developed a strong trust, that is, a strong faith in God's providential care for Israel. On the other hand, the children of Israel, whose conversation has been with Moses and his proxy Aaron, have definitely not arrived at this same level of trust, either in Moses or in God, even though they have been a party to every miracle so far.

Leaving the Red Sea, Israel soon enters the "wilderness of Sin" (Exo. 16:1). When privation begins to afflict them in the form of hunger or thirst, their thoughts turn back to imagined better times in Egypt. They forget all the harsh cruelties that accompanied those "better" times. One has to guess that some of the loudest spokesmen for this nostalgia had suffered less, through currying favor with the Egyptians, and were probably complicit in the oppression of their kinfolk.

While Moses is focused on heaven and God's providential destiny, the grumblers are focused on the momentary needs of the flesh. Of course, the needs of the flesh are important, but God is able to care for those needs easily. He tells Moses that He will provide a daily allotment of bread, but with the stipulation that the congregation was not to try to hoard extra provisions, but must trust in the Lord's *daily* provision. Israel must believe that God will still be with them each and every morning when they arise and step out of their tents. This is referred to as a "testing" by God (Exo. 16:4).

When Moses and Aaron relay God's instructions regarding the manna, they repeatedly emphasize the people's grumbling. Although the complaints come to Moses and Aaron, they point out that this grumbling is ultimately against God their provider (Exo. 16:8). At this point, God appears in glory and declares:

> "I have heard the grumbling of the people of Israel. Say to them, 'At twilight you shall eat meat, and in the morning you shall be filled with bread. Then you shall know that I am the LORD your God'" (Exo. 16:12).

That evening quail begin falling out of the sky. In the morning a frost-like substance had fallen on the ground all around their camp. This "manna", (or 'what is it?'), could be easily turned into various types of bread. From the sounds of it, manna was quite tasty. "It was like coriander seed, white, and the taste of it was like wafers made with honey" (Exo. 16:31).

The Testing

As we saw, Israel was given specific instructions for the collection of the manna. Further, we saw that God refers to this as a testing (Exo. 16:4). Unfortunately, not everyone passes this test well: "But they did not listen to Moses. Some left part of it till the morning, and it bred worms and stank" (Exo. 16:20). Included in the instructions was a provision for the Sabbath, in which there was to be no manna collected. Thus, the children of Israel were instructed to gather twice as much the day before (Friday morning), and the saved portion would not rot or stink. "On the seventh day some of the people went out to gather, but they found none" (Exo. 16:27).

Having faith in tomorrow's rosy disposition is not that easy. I suppose this testing could easily be referred to as God training up the people's faith. I keep insurance on my house and on my vehicle. I have made provisions for my eventual death should the Lord tarry. I back up my computer and my phone. But when God gives specific instructions, it is smart to trust His word and obey. Faith will grow with each promise fulfilled, in this case, every morning.

The main point we should glean from this is that God was forcing Moses and the Israelites to trust Him and Him alone.

While Moses seems to have come to full faith in God, the Israelites are still hedging their bets, to their detriment.

Keeping a Remembrance

While the children of Israel are focused on the relentless trudging through the wilderness, and Moses is focused on the promises that lie ahead, God knows that this formative period will pass, and it will be important to remember the lessons of the wilderness, many of which are yet to come. And God gives Moses specific instructions:

> Moses said, "This is what the LORD has commanded: 'Let an omer of it be kept throughout your generations, so that they may see the bread with which I fed you in the wilderness, when I brought you out of the land of Egypt'" (Exo. 16:32).

Remembrance is a strong reinforcement of lessons learned through difficult times of testing. The hope is that those same difficult times of testing will not have to be repeated. In the same way, Moses will teach the Israelites songs recounting their journeys, which are meant to be sung often so that coming generations will have the lessons of the wilderness drilled into them. The final book of Moses, Deuteronomy, is a retelling of the history of Israel's Exodus up to the moment of their entry into the land of Caanan. This text is specifically meant to be read and copied by their kings in the time to come (Deut. 17:18-20).

In addition, Moses added a second instruction meant for all the people:

"At the end of every seven years, at the set time in the year of release, at the Feast of Booths, when all Israel comes to appear before the LORD your God at the place that he will choose, you shall read this law before all Israel in their hearing" (Deut. 31:10-11).

When Moses says "this law," he means the book of Deuteronomy, which, as mentioned, includes a lengthy retelling of the history of the Exodus.

Discussion Points:

1. As hunger began to gnaw at their bellies, it seems that the Israelites began to have a selective memory of their time in Egypt. Moses' time in Egypt was largely one of great privilege. How does he maintain a focus on God's vision and not on former good times?

2. Clearly there were voices of complaint within the camp. These voices had a corrosive effect upon the congregation. How well does Moses counter the complaints?

3. God "tests" the people, requiring them to have faith for every day's provision. Does this seem to be a pass/fail testing, or some sort of training?

4. God emphasizes the need for remembrance. We have these Scriptures as a result. Discuss the importance of remembrance.

Application:

1. We all have our bad days when the past seems so much better than today. How do you refocus on God's good plans ahead, (I assume that God has a good plan for your life)?

2. Who do you listen to regularly? Is their council uplifting, heaven bound or earth bound?

3. Have you ever felt tested by God?

4. How important is it to remember the things that God has done in your life? Has there been prophetic words spoken over you? How does this help you moving forward? Can you share an example?

Moses and the Yoke of Fire

CHAPTER 8:   WATERS OF MERIBAH

So Moses cried to the LORD, "What shall I do with this people? They are almost ready to stone me" (Exo. 17:4).

Reading: **Exodus 17:1-16 & 19:1-8**

A Rock of Offense

We have been tracing the remarkable growth of Moses' faith, but side by side with his faith, it seems that the children of Israel, despite so many wonders on their behalf, are still not trusting that this journey into the unknown is a smart idea. Upon leaving the Red Sea behind, they camp a Marah, which has water, but the water is not drinkable. The people complain to Moses, so Moses talks to God, who shows him a particular log, which he throws into the water, making the water drinkable.

They are now traveling in barren lands where water is scarce. They travel to Elim with plentiful water, but then on to Rephidim by way of the wilderness of Sin. At Rephidim, once again, they find no water. Despite God's miraculous provision on every leg of their journey so-far, the people do not look up to heaven for help, but come, once again, to Moses. They are angry and demanding water. In an attempt to redirect their focus, Moses suggests, "Why do you quarrel with me? Why do you test the LORD?" (Exo. 17:2).

Once again, the accusation comes out, "Why did you bring us up out of Egypt, to kill us and our children and our livestock with thirst?" (Exo. 17:3). The faithful leader is wearing thin. His query to God reflects a dangerous turn, "What shall I do with this people?" (Exo. 17:4). What is remarkable is that the Scriptures show us, not just the highs of our great forebears, but their moments of failure. In this case, Moses has stepped into the martyrs' role. "What shall *I* do?"

God tells him to strike the rock at Horeb with his shepherd's rod (Exo. 17:6). Striking the rock, abundant water pours out. "And he called the name of the place Massah and Meribah, because of the quarreling of the people of Israel, and because they tested the LORD by saying, 'Is the LORD among us or not?'" (Exo. 17:7). Meribah, which means 'place of contention', is the name given to another place as well, where this same story will be reenacted with worse results.

More Bumps in the Road

Exodus chapter 17 ends with Israel's first battle. Israel is still camped at Rephidim when Amalekites appear armed for war. Israel is a nation of former slaves. They have no experience in warfare and are poorly armed. On top of this, Amalek was a grandson of Esau, making the Amalekites cousins to Israel. But the die is cast, Moses tells Joshua to choose men to fight for Israel and prepare (Exo. 17:9).

Meanwhile, Moses goes to the hill overlooking the ensuing battle to raise the shepherd's rod calling for God's help. Staff raised, Joshua and Israel prevail against Amalek. But when he became tired, Moses lowered his staff. At this, Amalek prevailed. Thus, as Moses became weary, Aaron and Hur sit

Moses down and hold his arms high until Amalek is thoroughly beaten (Exo. 17:12-13). Moses erects an altar on the spot, and calls the name of it "The LORD Is My Banner" (Exo. 17:15).

God is very unhappy with Amalek. "Write this as a memorial in a book and recite it in the ears of Joshua, that I will utterly blot out the memory of Amalek from under heaven" (Exo. 17:14). In time to come, Israel's first king Saul will go afoul of God when he fails to complete the annihilation of the Amalekites and everything associated with them (1Sam. 28:16-19).

Bourne on Eagle's Wings

Moving on, Moses and the children of Israel finally arrive at the "Mountain of God." This is the same mountain where Moses met God in the burning bush. They have not arrived here by accident, but have come according to God's instructions to Moses delivered in this very place, "when you have brought the people out of Egypt, you shall serve God on this mountain" (Exo. 3:12). Despite all of the bumps in the road, Moses has done his job.

As the people make camp, Moses goes up on the mountain to meet the Lord:

> The LORD called to him out of the mountain, saying, "Thus you shall say to the house of Jacob, and tell the people of Israel:
>
> "'You yourselves have seen what I did to the Egyptians, and how I bore you on eagles' wings and brought you to myself. Now therefore, if you will indeed obey my

voice and keep my covenant, you shall be
my treasured possession among all peoples,
for all the earth is mine; and you shall be to
me a kingdom of priests and a holy nation.'

"These are the words that you shall speak
to the people of Israel" (Exo. 19:3-6).

Moses conveys everything that the Lord has told him to the
elders of the people of Israel, and the people answer, "All that
the LORD has spoken we will do" (Exo. 19:8).

Discussion Points:

1. Given all that God has done for Israel so far, why do you suppose the people are so contentious with Moses?

2. Moses seems to be increasingly feeling the weight of the yoke placed on him at the burning bush. Is there something he should be doing to make the weight of responsibility lighter?

3. God is incredibly upset with Amalek; more so than with later attackers. Why do you suppose this is? How does this align with our instruction to "love our enemies?"

4. God has bourn his people "on eagle's wings" to the "mountain of God." Why do you suppose they have been brought to this place?

Application:

1. It is easy to say, "Do not fear," but not always easy to do so in practice. The greater sin is pointing fingers to fix blame. Have you had to struggle with these feelings? How did you shake the feeling?

2. Sometimes we feel crushed by the yoke placed on us by various responsibilities. Discuss ways to cope with responsibility without shirking the job.

3. Sometimes forgiveness and loving our enemies is hard to do. Is vengeance better in our hands or in Gods?

4. Have you ever felt that God has been directing your life? Do you imagine that He has something to teach you that you have yet to grasp?

CHAPTER 9:   THE MOUNTAIN OF GOD

Moses said to the people, "Do not fear, for God has come to test you, that the fear of him may be before you, that you may not sin." The people stood far off, while Moses drew near to the thick darkness where God was (Exo. 20:20-21).

Reading: **Exodus 20:1-21; 32:1-35;**

and Exodus 33:12 through 34:9

The Encounter

The presence of God is so strong on the "mountain of God" that now it wasn't a bush that appeared to be burning, but the entire top of the mountain was covered in fire and thick smoke. Where Moses had approached the burning bush before, he goes immediately to converse with God in the fire. Although it seems that the warning should be unnecessary, God warns Moses that the people must not approach. Chapter 20 begins with God Himself speaking the words of the Ten Commandments aloud to the gathered congregation. Their response was to draw away:

> Now when all the people saw the thunder
> and the flashes of lightning and the sound
> of the trumpet and the mountain smoking,
> the people were afraid and trembled, and
> they stood far off and said to Moses, "You
> speak to us, and we will listen; but do not
> let God speak to us, lest we die" (Exo.
> 20:18-19).

While the people keep their distance, Moses draws near and receives the Ten Commandments and other statutes. These he writes down for the people and shares it with the leaders. He then takes the leaders to meet God directly:

> Then Moses and Aaron, Nadab, and Abihu,
> and seventy of the elders of Israel went up,
> and they saw the God of Israel. There was
> under his feet as it were a pavement of sap-
> phire stone, like the very heaven for clear-
> ness. And he did not lay his hand on the
> chief men of the people of Israel; they be-
> held God, and ate and drank (Exo. 24:9-11).

After the people have received instructions, including the Ten Commandments and several other statutes, and the leaders have come into the powerful presence of God. This presence is so powerful that it seems that the chief men of Israel spent their time gazing at the floor for fear of looking up.

Moses is ready to go up onto the mountain for forty days and forty nights. Here he will receive yoke Ten Commandments written on stone by the finger of God, instructions for build-ing the tabernacle and the articles for worship, details on how to carry out daily offerings, and many more statutes. Alone with him is his assistant Joshua, who will wait at the base of the mountain.

The Golden Calf

Chapter 32 begins with Aaron creating a golden calf for the children of Israel. The Hebrew doesn't make it clear that Aaron is intending to create a different god or gods[2], so we could perhaps give him a pass on the violation of the first of the Ten Commandments, but this is a clear violation of the second commandment. Moses hasn't been gone forty days, and the promises of the people have been tossed aside. Moreover, it is Aaron at the head of the pack.

If we give the congregation a pass on the first commandment, the violation of the second commandment amounts to further distancing themselves from God. As we saw, when confronting God at the mountain, all the people backed a way, and then asked Moses to talk to God and then relay the message to them. By creating an image of their own choosing, they are, in essence, creating their own image of God according to their own wishes. The text indicates that the celebration of this event is more Mardi Gras carnival, with all of its attendant debauchery, than a Synagogue service.

God informs Moses of what is happening down in the camp, and declares His intention of putting an end to the people. He further indicates that He will make a great nation of Moses instead:

---

[2] "Gods" plural, in Hebrew, can be used to emphasize importance, as in the supreme god.

> "I have seen this people, and behold, it is a stiff-necked people. Now therefore let me alone, that my wrath may burn hot against them and I may consume them, in order that I may make a great nation of you" (Exo. 32:9-10).

There on the mountain, we see a remarkable development in Moses' character. Rather than letting God alone to consume them, he intercedes for Israel:

> "O LORD, why does your wrath burn hot against your people, whom you have brought out of the land of Egypt with great power and with a mighty hand? Why should the Egyptians say, 'With evil intent did he bring them out, to kill them in the mountains and to consume them from the face of the earth'? Turn from your burning anger and relent from this disaster against your people. Remember Abraham, Isaac, and Israel, your servants, to whom you swore by your own self, and said to them, 'I will multiply your offspring as the stars of heaven, and all this land that I have promised I will give to your offspring, and they shall inherit it forever'" (Exo. 32:11-13).

This will not be the last time that Moses is called upon to stand between God's wrath and the children of Israel. The text doesn't give us deep insight into how God feels about this particular intervention, but it would surely align itself favorably with the forgiving aspect of God's character. I imagine that God is actually pleased that Moses is beginning to grasp

His character and reflect it back forcefully in the face of His declared intention. Is this, in fact, a test of his character?

Standing on the mountain, the extent to which Israel has strayed is not fully apparent to Moses. When he and Joshua return to the camp, he is so stunned by what he sees that he throws down the two tablets that God has written upon, breaking them into pieces. God does relent from annihilating Israel, but that does not mean that they escape unscathed. First, Moses calls those who are loyal to him, the Levites, and instructs them:

> "Thus says the LORD God of Israel, 'Put
> your sword on your side each of you, and
> go to and fro from gate to gate throughout
> the camp, and each of you kill his brother
> and his companion and his neighbor'" (Exo.
> 32:27).

They scatter throughout the camp to kill the obvious offenders, about three-thousand men, and likely a large number of women as well (Exo. 32:28). Again, Moses goes before God to ask for forgiveness on behalf of the people, God agrees but not without further cleansing, sending a plague upon those who remain (Exo. 32:31-35).

You're Glory Must Go With Us

And now, it is the time for inheritance. God tells Moses that it is time for the people to go up into the land that He has promised to give them, and that His angel will go before them to drive out the inhabitants. In the next chapter, God clarifies that He intends to send His angel with them, but that He Himself will not go with them (Exo. 33:2-3). Moses is unhappy.

He sets himself to intercession, imploring God based on his own faithfulness. He presses God until God says, "My presence will go with you, and I will give you rest" (Exo. 33:14). Now that Moses has achieved his purpose, you might assume that he would leave it at that, but Moses continues to press for even more assurance of God's presence. Finally, he asks, "Please show me your glory" (Exo. 33:18). What we are witnessing is Moses drawing closer and closer to God with great respect, but powerful boldness, indicating how thoroughly he has become familiar, in a true sense and not in a vulgar sense, with God's Spirit.

Moses cuts two more tablets and returns to the mountain to restore the two tablets broken after the incident of the golden calf. There on the mountain, God does as Moses has asked. He places Moses in a cleft of the rock and passes before him in full glory, proclaiming,

> "The LORD, the LORD, a God merciful and gracious, slow to anger, and abounding in steadfast love and faithfulness, keeping steadfast love for thousands, forgiving iniquity and transgression and sin, but who will by no means clear the guilty, visiting the iniquity of the fathers on the children and the children's children, to the third and the fourth generation" (Exo. 34:6-7).

Moses' response is to bow his head and worship. However, not one to lose an opportunity, Moses renews his request, "If now I have found favor in your sight, O Lord, please let the Lord go in the midst of us, for it is a stiff-necked people, and pardon our iniquity and our sin, and take us for your inheritance" (Exo. 34:9).

At the end of this second forty days on the mountain of God, Moses returns with the skin of his face radiating so much light that Aaron and the people were afraid to approach him (Exo. 34:2-30). Nevertheless, Moses calls Aaron and the leaders to him and then relays to them all everything that God has told him on the mountain. After this, Moses covered his face.

It appears that while the people are distancing themselves from God, Moses is drawing ever closer to God, and that his very presence among the people is now radiating that very presence, the presence that the children of Israel have been trying to get some distance from. Our God reaches out with a relentless desire.

The book of Exodus continues with the instructions for creating the tabernacle. In chapter 40, the tabernacle is erected and the articles of worship set in place. "And Moses was not able to enter the tent of meeting because the cloud settled on it, and the glory of the LORD filled the tabernacle" (Exo. 40:35). Henceforth, God's presence will travel with the tabernacle until it reaches the promised land, just as Moses had asked.

Discussion Points:

1. Why does Moses draw near? Why do the children of Israel retreat?

2. God offers to make of Moses a great nation, instead of Israel. Why does Moses intercede so fervently for the children of Israel?

3. Why is Moses so adamant that God's glory, and not just a representative angel, stay with Israel?

4. Moses truly does become like God to his people (Exo. 4:16) when he appears with his face shining with the glory. Why does he cover his face?

Application:

1. Have you ever experienced the thick presence of the Holy Spirit? Were you drawn to it or repelled?

2. Sometimes prayers of intercession war against the desires of our flesh, as when asked to pray for someone who has used us in an unjust manner. How easy is it to pray at those times?

3. Have you had a powerful spiritual experienced and were not sure if it was holy or unholy? What happened to bring the experience? How do you discern the holy from the unholy?

4. Psalm 82:6 says "You are gods, sons of the Most High, all of you." How well do you feel that you model God's character to others?

80.   Moses and the Yoke of Fire

CHAPTER 10:   STRANGE FIRE

> Now Nadab and Abihu, the sons of Aaron, each took his censer and put fire in it and laid incense on it and offered unauthorized fire before the LORD, which he had not commanded them. And fire came out from before the LORD and consumed them, and they died before the LORD (Lev. 10:1-2).

Reading: Leviticus 10:1-20

Nadab and Abihu

The book of Leviticus is mostly a listing of various laws covering a wide variety of issues, most prominently, how to come before the Lord and offer sacrifices. The one exception is chapter ten, which relays the offering of "unauthorized fire," or "strange fire" as the King James translates the passage. We don't know exactly what Aaron's two sons did, but we do know that they did not follow the rules governing the offering of incense. It is widely assumed that alcohol was involved as the incident concludes with the injunction to Aaron: "Drink no wine or strong drink, you or your sons with you, when you go into the tent of meeting, lest you die. It shall be a statute forever throughout your generations" (Lev. 10:9).

From the point of view of ethics, there are two ways to view this infraction. First, we could say that the two young men had violated specific rules and were punished for their disobedience. I suspect that most of us naturally assume this to be the case.

But there is another way to look at this event, particularly if excessive drinking was involved. If the two young men came before the Lord to offer incense in a giddy state, offering a humorous, but disrespectful offering, then their death by the fire of God was not punishment for violating the rules, but a warning to all priests who come into the sanctuary to treat the Lord's offerings with respect. By focusing on the activity and thinking of how to have fun with it, Nadab and Abihu failed to realize that they were about to enter into the manifest presence of God. The activity of the incense offering is insignificant compared to communion it afforded them, coming into an intimate interaction with God.

I Will be Sanctified

To his horror, Aaron's two oldest boys have just died, killed by the fire of God. Moses steps in, "This is what the LORD has said: 'Among those who are near me I will be sanctified, and before all the people I will be glorified'" (Lev. 10:3). This reinforces the second conclusion above, the two young men failed to recognize the gravity of coming into the presence of the Lord. The failure to render glory to God is the same issue that will trip up Moses and Aaron at the waters of Meribah-kadesh (chapter 14).

Moses further instructs Aaron and his two younger sons that they may not mourn in the customary manner. These deaths were caused by their failure to honor God, so, as priests the three must give full respect to God and His will in punishing the two offenders. They must honor God's decision by not mourning as custom would normally call for. However, Moses tells them, "let your brothers, the whole house of Israel, bewail the burning that the LORD has kindled" (Lev. 10:6).

At the heart of it, Moses, and thus God, was teaching Aaron, as well as Eleazar and Ithamar, his surviving sons, "You are to distinguish between the holy and the common, and between the unclean and the clean, and you are to teach the people of Israel all the statutes that the LORD has spoken to them by Moses" (Lev 10:10-11). This ultimately came down to those places, activities, and articles of worship which drew the presence of the Lord.

A Goat Not Eaten

Following this, Moses instructs Aaron, Eleazar and Ithamar to carry on with the proper sacrifice for the sin offering, while they remain secluded in the tent of meeting for a week. The thigh of a sacrificial goat is waved before the Lord as a sin offering, and then was to be eaten by the priests before the next day. Anything that remains was to be burned.

Moses leaves to explain things to the camp waiting outside for news. He likely had to calm some nerves in the camp as well. Upon returning to the tent of meeting, Moses "diligently inquired" about the goat of the offering. The two sons had not eaten it, and so the entire offering had been burned up. Flushed with anger, Moses demands,

> "Why have you not eaten the sin offering
> in the place of the sanctuary, since it is a
> thing most holy and has been given to you

> that you may bear the iniquity of the con-
> gregation, to make atonement for them be-
> fore the LORD? Behold, its blood was not
> brought into the inner part of the sanctuary.
> You certainly ought to have eaten it in the
> sanctuary, as I commanded" (Lev. 10:17-
> 18).

Focused on taking care of the things of God, Moses has failed to recognize that these three, for better or for worse, are still struggling with the grief of losing sons and brothers. Aaron steps in to suggest, "Behold, today they have offered their sin offering and their burnt offering before the LORD, and yet such things as these have happened to me! If I had eaten the sin offering today, would the LORD have approved?" (Lev. 10:19).

In respect for the Lord, the three have laid aside the traditional rites of mourning, but they are grieving nevertheless. Recognizing the wisdom in Aaron's reply, Moses holds his peace. The rites of the sanctuary come down to an interchange between the priests, Aaron and his sons as representatives of all of Israel, and God. Their worship is a sign of heartfelt respect. Despite carefully laid out procedures, these were never intended to create perfect mechanical activities, but to set the mood and focus the mind to meet the invisible God. The death of two young priests was a very hard lesson, but we must assume, a necessary lesson.

Discussion Points:

1. At this point, it is useful to stop and imagine what Nadab and Abihu's strange fire might have been and discuss what might have caused the incident.

2. God's response was quick and severe. What was so upsetting to God? Why do you suppose death was called for in this instance?

3. Moses cautions Aaron and his two surviving sons not to mourn in the traditional manner. This is done to respect God's decision. This would have stirred up strong emotions in the three. How is it that they are willing to listen to Moses and respect his instructions?

4. The rules are bent somewhat, without any disrespect for the Lord, Aaron and his sons are given the room to struggle. Discuss this, and Moses' struggle with their failure to follow the rules.

Application:

1. Have you ever been in a situation in church or other worship environment in which you thought the atmosphere had become "unholy?"

2. Why do you think that we seem to get away with much looser standards today, than did Nadab and Abihu?

3. Sometimes, doing the right thing in emotionally difficult times is so hard that we need someone to guide us through trying times. Can you think of a specific time when this became necessary for you?

4. Sometimes it is difficult to know when it is OK to bend the rules. Are there situations that have come up for you, in which it is difficult to know what is acceptable and what cannot be done?

CHAPTER 11:   THE YOKE

> Moses said to the LORD, "Why have you dealt ill with your servant? And why have I not found favor in your sight, that you lay the burden of all this people on me?" (Num. 11:11).

Reading: Numbers 11:1-35

Sharing the Load

One thing about slavery is that the uncertainty of life is done away with. Life may not be pleasant, but there is always the knowledge that there will be food from the master's scraps and the work is regular. Living in the wilderness where there is little food or water and the future is uncertain, life can be frightening for a former population of slaves, leading to the desire to return to Egypt. Despite all of the good things that God has done for them, their rebellions have earned them plagues of various kinds. The children of Israel are still not sure about this Moses and his God.

As they break camp at the mountain of God, to once more step into the unknown, their minds travel back to foods of Egypt, and to the security of their monotonous life there. At each new campsite, complaints begin to arise, causing God to send fire into the outer parts of the camp (Num. 11:1). Still the grumbling increases, and there is more weeping for the nostalgia of yesterday. "Moses heard the people weeping throughout their clans, everyone at the door of his tent. And the anger of the LORD blazed hotly, and Moses was displeased" (Num. 11:10). And so, Moses complains to the Lord: "I am not able to carry all this people alone; the burden is too heavy for me. If you will treat me like this, kill me at once, if I find favor in your sight, that I may not see my wretchedness" (Num. 11:15). God has no intention of killing Moses. Instead, he directs Moses to gather the seventy elders to the tent of meeting. "I will take some of the Spirit that is on you and put it on them, and they shall bear the burden of the people with you, so that you may not bear it yourself alone" (Num. 11:17).

When relaying God's instructions to the elders, Moses adds, "Consecrate yourselves for tomorrow, and you shall eat meat, for you have wept in the hearing of the LORD, saying, 'Who will give us meat to eat? For it was better for us in Egypt.' Therefore the LORD will give you meat, and you shall eat" (Num. 11:18). Not just a little meat, but so much meat that they will all become sick of meat, "until it comes out at your nostrils" (Num. 11:20).

> So Moses went out and told the people the words of the LORD. And he gathered seventy men of the elders of the people and placed them around the tent. Then the LORD came down in the cloud and spoke to him, and took some of the Spirit that was on him and put it on the seventy elders. And as soon as the Spirit rested on them, they prophesied. But they did not continue doing it (Num. 11:24-25).

You will recall that per Jethro's suggestion, Moses has made the elders active participants in resolving disputes and other matters of judgement, but this is another matter. The Spirit of the living God is being dispersed to the seventy elders, so that heavenly discernment and wisdom will be with them to help to ferret out and calm the rebellious voices.

Eldad and Medad

Two men had remained in the camp, meaning they were meant to come as a part of the gathering of the elders. When the Spirit fell on the elders gathered around the tent of meeting, it also fell on these two, Eldad and Medad. The text says that, "they prophesied in the camp" (Num. 11:26). Exactly what this looked like we don't know. Perhaps they spoke in tongues, perhaps they began to make prophetic announcements or maybe they just shouted "Alleluia!" at the top of their lungs. Whatever the case, it was shocking enough that someone quickly ran to tell Moses about it.

Joshua, Moses faithful assistant, jealous to protect the special dignity of his mentor, exclaimed, "My lord Moses, stop them" (Num. 11:28). Moses sees this event differently. This is something that God is doing, "Are you jealous for my sake? Would that all the LORD's people were prophets, that the LORD would put his Spirit on them!" (Num. 11:29).

This move of God is one which will increase the presence of God with all of the people through their leadership. This is a good thing. God's dignity is the important factor that is being elevated in this moment. If Moses' personal dignity is diminished somewhat in the process, which is not likely, it is an acceptable sacrifice; in fact, for Moses at this point it is a welcome sacrifice. Now the focus will be on God where it belongs.

More Quail

Previously, because of the complaints of the people, God had sent quail to them in the wilderness of Sin at the same time that He began to surround the camp with the manna. This is a more serious incident, however, as the people have been fed with manna for quite some time, God appears to have less patience with them.

A wind coming off of the sea brings quail. Large numbers of quail begin falling from the sky all around the camp. The people rush out to gather piles of quail. "While the meat was yet between their teeth, before it was consumed, the anger of the LORD was kindled against the people, and the LORD struck down the people with a very great plague" (Num. 11:33).

Psalm 78 gives some context. It suggests that, "They tested God in their heart by demanding the food they craved" (Psa. 78:18). The implication is that the people wanted God to serve them according to their prescribed desires. Remember that Numbers 11 begins with the people treating the manna with disgust. Psalm 78 refers to the manna as "the bread of the angels" (Psa. 78:25). God has given them heavenly food, but they would rather return to the slave's portion.

Further, this psalm describes God's reaction as angry. "Therefore, when the LORD heard, he was full of wrath; a fire was kindled against Jacob; his anger rose against Israel, because they did not believe in God and did not trust his saving power" (Psa. 78:21-22). The consequences are swift and devastating. "But before they had satisfied their craving, while the food was still in their mouths, the anger of God rose against them, and he killed the strongest of them and laid low the young men of Israel" (Psa. 78:30-31).

The main point we should glean from this is that God was forcing Moses and the Israelites to trust Him and Him alone. While Moses seems to have come to full faith in God, the Israelites are still hedging their bets, to their detriment.

Discussion Points:

1. The uncertainty of the wilderness has caused the children of Israel to look backwards and see their former life in positive terms. What are they failing to see in this desire to return to their former life?

2. Where the people see uncertainty, Moses seems confident. Why is Moses so confident?

3. Eldad and Medad seemed to be expressing a spiritual demeaner that didn't accord with the expected norm. While several seemed offended by their outburst, Moses welcomes it. What do you suppose the expression looked like and why is Moses happy with it?

4. The children of Israel beg for meat, and so God sends quail in such a great quantity that many become sick and die. What is God telling the people in this instance?

Application:

1. Have you faced uncertainty that has caused you to want to retreat to a less than perfect safety?

2. Are there things in your spiritual life that give you strength to challenge difficulties and reach for an uncertain destiny?

3. Sometimes we come in contact with other churches or believers whose behavior does not accord well with what we have been taught to believe. How much grace are you able to extend in these circumstances?

4. Sometimes getting what you want is a bad idea. Think of an instance where you got what you wanted, but wished that you hadn't?

94.   Moses and the Yoke of Fire

CHAPTER 12:   COLD FEET

So they brought to the people of Israel a bad report of the land that they had spied out, saying, "The land, through which we have gone to spy it out, is a land that devours its inhabitants, and all the people that we saw in it are of great height. And there we saw the Nephilim (the sons of Anak, who come from the Nephilim), and we seemed to ourselves like grasshoppers, and so we seemed to them" (Num. 13:32-33).

Reading: **Numbers 14:1-45**

Spies Sent Out

Rather than go up directly into the land that Israel is meant to take possession of, the leaders suggest that Moses should have the land checked first. Moses accepts their hesitancy and spies are sent to spy out the land. Ten of the spies are fearful of the inhabitants of the land and convince the people that it will be impossible drive out the land's inhabitants. Caleb tries to intervene suggesting that they were all well able to take the land (Num. 13:30), but the fearful report wins the day.

That night terrified wailing is heard throughout the camp. As the dawn light creeps across the camp, so do the angry voices, "Why is the LORD bringing us into this land, to fall by the sword? Our wives and our little ones will become a prey. Would it not be better for us to go back to Egypt?" (Num 14:3). Plans are made to elect a new leader and return to captivity. At this, Joshua and Caleb, spies with a different view, stand up to protest:

> "The land, which we passed through to spy it out, is an exceedingly good land. If the LORD delights in us, he will bring us into this land and give it to us, a land that flows with milk and honey. Only do not rebel against the LORD. And do not fear the people of the land, for they are bread for us. Their protection is removed from them, and the LORD is with us; do not fear them" (Num 14:7-9).

These brave words are met with contempt, as the people begin gathering stones with which to stone them. The execution is interrupted as the glory of the Lord descends. Out of this glory cloud, the Lord speaks to Moses:

> "How long will this people despise me? And how long will they not believe in me, in spite of all the signs that I have done among them? I will strike them with the pestilence and disinherit them, and I will make of you a nation greater and mightier than they" (Num. 14:12).

Once again, God offers to eliminate Moses' burden and make a new nation starting with himself, perhaps with Joshu, Caleb,

Aaron and his sons. I assume that their families would be included. Wives are often be ignored in the Biblical narrative, but they would be very important to any future. As we saw in the last chapter, Moses has asked for his burden, his burning yoke of responsibility to be taken away. He thinks better of it this time.

Intercession for Israel

Moses' reaction is also quite different from the self-righteous anger exhibited by his ancestor Levi, and as his own approach in times past. The Lord's offer to make a nation of Moses to replace the recalcitrant nation of Israel does not please him. First, he argues that killing the people will convince the Egyptians and the inhabitants of the land of Canaan that "the LORD was not able to bring this people into the land that he swore to give to them" (Num. 14:16). And then he asks for grace according to God's own self-identification:

> "And now, please let the power of the Lord be great as you have promised, saying, 'The LORD is slow to anger and abounding in steadfast love, forgiving iniquity and transgression, but he will by no means clear the guilty, visiting the iniquity of the fathers on the children, to the third and the fourth generation.' Please pardon the iniquity of this people, according to the greatness of your steadfast love, just as you have forgiven this people, from Egypt until now"
> (Num. 14:17-19).

Moses is becoming attuned to God in such a remarkable way, that he is able to stand before the Almighty and say, "No, don't do that… it is not Your character to do it so." He even quotes God's self-description. To this, God answers, "I have pardoned, according to your word" (Num. 14:20). Unfortunately, the second part of God's self-description quoted above is "I will by no means clear the guilty" (Num. 14:18). None of the rebellious, all of those who have witnessed the miracles of God, but have lost faith in the saving power of the hosts of heaven, will enter the land of promise. All will die in the wilderness. The ten spies who had brought a bad report, thus leading Israel to lose faith and rebel, immediately died of plague (Num. 14:37). Joshua and Caleb, the two faithful spies, were spared and go on to enter the land of Canaan.

A False Repentance

The children of Israel are misunderstanding the problem, the difference is between doing what they think, including what they think God wants them to do, and following the Lord. Having been told that their faithlessness is the issue, they decide that the solution is to go up to fight the Amalekites. "Here we are. We will go up to the place that the LORD has promised, for we have sinned" (Num. 14:40). This is an attempt to repent and rectify their sin. But to rectify the sin, they must put away their own self-will and lean into God. By deciding on their own how to solve the problem, they have only compounded the problem. They have not repented in that they have not turned away from the self-reliance that has put them on the wrong footing with God.

The Israelites have seen miracle upon miracle performed on their behalf, but they still fear the conflict ahead, they still have no faith in God's care for them. Chagrined by Moses' rebuke, they decide to go up against the Amalekites despite their fear, but now they are stepping into battle with no faith in God's hand of protection.

The direction of the Lord is to turn away from the Amalekites towards the wilderness. And so, Moses answers,

> "Why now are you transgressing the command of the LORD, when that will not succeed? Do not go up, for the Lord is not among you, lest you be struck down before your enemies" (Num. 14:41-2).

Once again, the impetuous children of Israel ignore Moses and go into the hills to challenge the Amalekites only to be routed. Moses and arc of the covenant stay in camp, knowing there will be more losses to mourn.

Discussion Points:

1. We see Moses' faith set against the faith of the children of Israel. Once again, a lack of faith causes disaster. Place yourself in the situation that these former slaves are in. Where would your faith be?

2. The relationship that Moses has with God is so much closer than those who follow him. Discuss the factors that may be guiding his growing intimacy with God.

3. Moses argues to change God's mind. Is Moses sensing that God desires something other than His stated course of action, or is Moses asking God to choose a path that is not God's first choice?

4. Having been disciplined for turning away from the battle, the logical choice is to gather courage and go. Why does Moses (and God) say 'No'?

Application:

1. Our faith choices in life are rarely as clear as the choices portrayed here in Scripture. Have there been times when you felt your faith faltered? What may have been the reason?

2. Are there things that you could be doing to deepen your intimacy with God? Are there people around you who seem more intimate with God?

3. Is it possible that you can change God mind, or at least what He is allowing you to choose? Have there been prayers that you are glad that God did not answer?

4. How important is your faith in making difficult decisions? Do your fears sometimes override your faith?

102.   Moses and the Yoke of Fire

CHAPTER 13:   SWALLOWED

"But if the LORD creates something new, and the ground opens its mouth and swallows them up with all that belongs to them, and they go down alive into Sheol, then you shall know that these men have despised the LORD" (Num. 16:30).

Reading: Numbers 16:1-50

Korah's Rebellion

On the heels of the rebellion at the threshold of Canaan land, Korah, a Levite, along with On, Dathan and Abiram lead a rebellion of 250 leaders against the leadership of Moses and Aaron, challenging, "You have gone too far! For all in the congregation are holy, every one of them, and the LORD is among them. Why then do you exalt yourselves above the assembly of the LORD?" (Num. 16:3).

Moses' response is to fall on his face. The symbolism could indicate humility, but could also indicate his need to hear God's voice in the matter. In any case, he rises to speak with a clear prophetic confidence, "In the morning the LORD will show who is his, and who is holy, and will bring him near to him. The one whom he chooses he will bring near to him"

(Num. 16:5). He instructs them to bring censers for burning incense to the tent of meeting in the morning. Moses boldly proclaims the purpose, "the man whom the LORD chooses shall be the holy one" (Num. 16:7).

> And Moses said to Korah, "Hear now, you sons of Levi: is it too small a thing for you that the God of Israel has separated you from the congregation of Israel, to bring you near to himself, to do service in the tabernacle of the LORD and to stand before the congregation to minister to them, and that he has brought you near him, and all your brothers the sons of Levi with you? And would you seek the priesthood also? Therefore it is against the LORD that you and all your company have gathered together. What is Aaron that you grumble against him?" (Num. 16:8-11).

Notice that Moses is speaking with clear authority, and with total confidence in what will happen. Moses is particularly angry with the brazen attitude of these men. It is hard to surmise exactly what is eating at Moses, but it is clear that these men wish to have spiritual leadership, without the spiritual authority that comes from above.

Two of the ringleaders Dathan and Abiram had not come before him, so Moses sends to have them join the rest of the rebels. In defiance of his authority, they refuse to appear.

The Ground Opens Its Mouth

On the next morning, Korah and 250 leaders stand before Moses with their censers burning incense all around the tent of meeting. The congregation of Israel stands with them to see what will transpire. God tells Moses and Aaron to stand back. "Separate yourselves from among this congregation, that I may consume them in a moment" (Num. 16:21). As always, Moses and Aaron fall on their faces to ask for God's mercy.

And so, the Lord narrows the request, "Say to the congregation, Get away from the dwelling of Korah, Dathan, and Abiram" (Num. 16:24). Dathan and Abiram are standing before their tents with their families beside them when Moses arrives. After instructing those not directly involved to back away, he declares,

> "Hereby you shall know that the LORD has sent me to do all these works, and that it has not been of my own accord. If these men die as all men die, or if they are visited by the fate of all mankind, then the LORD has not sent me. But if the LORD creates something new, and the ground opens its mouth and swallows them up with all that belongs to them, and they go down alive into Sheol, then you shall know that these men have despised the LORD" (Num. 16:28-30).

This is an incredibly bold statement, on the order of Jesus telling Peter to go fishing, and the first fish caught will have a specific coin in its mouth (Matt. 17:27). The ground opens immediately, swallowing the men, their families and all that they had possessed. Everyone nearby, anxious to see how this bold proclamation will play out, turn and flee for their lives.

Fire from heaven comes down to consume Korah and the 250 men standing with their censers to burn incense which they have not been authorized to do. They have clearly not learned the lesson of Nadab and Abihu.

The Rebels' Holy Censers

As the smoke clears, God instructs Moses to have Eleazar the priest, Aaron's son, collect the censers out of the fire, "for they have become holy" (Num. 16:37). It does seem a strange turn of events, as the incense was being offered in an act of rebellion and those who rebelled were all destroyed by the fire of God. Nevertheless, God considers the censers which offered the incense to be holy. Eleazar is instructed to collect them and to have them hammered out flat to make a covering for the alter.

The congregation is unhappy. They were on the side of the rebels and accuse Moses and Aaron, "You have killed the people of the LORD" (Num. 16:41), when in fact the Lord killed the rebel leaders, not Moses. Once again, God offers to eliminate the entire rebellious lot of them. Again, Moses and Aaron fall on their faces before the Lord. Moses arises to tell Aaron to put fire from off the alter and incense into his censer. A plague has already begun. "And he stood between the dead and the living, and the plague was stopped" (Num. 16:48).

To settle the issue of priestly leadership, God instructs the leaders of each tribe to bring a representative staff to the tent of meeting (Num. 17:2). These staffs, along with Aaron's staff, each with the man's name on it, are placed in the tent of testimony overnight.

> On the next day Moses went into the tent of
> the testimony, and behold, the staff of Aa-
> ron for the house of Levi had sprouted and

put forth buds and produced blossoms, and
it bore ripe almonds (Num. 17:8).

This should put an end to all the grumbling, but it seems that there is always someone who, despite all of the plagues and fire from heaven, is willing and ready to step out and share their personal opinion and displeasure. The world seems to never run out of grumblers and back-biters.

Discussion Points:

1. Moses speaks with clear authority in dealing with the rebellion of Korah. Do you suppose that this confidence is from a momentary word of the Lord, a strong confidence in the Lord, or both?

2. Moses shows anger at yet another rebellion. So many have died in plagues, unwise battles, and other effects of rebellion. Is this anger for the people or a personal indignity?

3. Discuss the similarities and dissimilarities between this event and the incident with Nadab and Abihu.

4. Having destroyed the 250 presumptuous worshipers, why is Eliasar instructed to treat their censers as holy?

Application:

1. Sometimes we will speak with clear authority. Are you able to discern when the authority is tradition, previous teaching, or a word from the Lord?

2. Often, we are angry, but the anger is not the anger of the Lord. How do you know the difference between righteous anger and self-righteous anger?

3. Is it still possible to offend God with an offering or other act of worship as we see in this account? What sort of worship that is not godly might we witness today?

4. What sort of worship, witness, or other godly act could be accepted by God, while the one making the offering is not blessed on account of it?

110.   Moses and the Yoke of Fire

CHAPTER 14:   ANOTHER MERIBAH

And the people quarreled with Moses and said, "Would that we had perished when our brothers perished before the LORD! Why have you brought the assembly of the LORD into this wilderness, that we should die here, both we and our cattle? And why have you made us come up out of Egypt to bring us to this evil place? It is no place for grain or figs or vines or pomegranates, and there is no water to drink" (Num. 20:3-5).

Reading: **Numbers 20:2-13 & 21:4-20**

The Rock of Offense

There are those moments when, while faithfully marching to the beat of heaven's drum, former stumbling blocks suddenly reappear. While we are busy looking to heaven, bang, our past has a nasty habit of sneaking up on us. If you will recall, self-righteous anger is the failure that mars Levi's legacy. Moses has done well in overcoming this tendency, but, suddenly he seems to stumble badly.

Just as previously in the wilderness of Sin, Israel again finds itself in a dry place with no water to drink. Referred to as the "wilderness of Zin", this may be the same wilderness or a separate portion of vast dry lands. Once again, the weight of responsibility is a heavy yoke on Moses' shoulders. Miriam has just died, as with so many others of those who came out of Egypt with him. Dry and parched, the angry voices cry out to their leader. As before, Moses goes before God to receive instructions. In this instance, God instructs Moses to "tell the rock" to bring forth water (Num. 20:8).

> Then Moses and Aaron gathered the assembly together before the rock, and he said to them, "Hear now, you rebels: shall we bring water for you out of this rock?" (Num. 20:10).

Moses strikes the rock. As before, the water pours forth from the rock. Some teaching has suggested that by striking the rock instead of speaking to it, Moses has failed, as if he failed to do the magic correctly. But look again at how Moses introduces this miracle: "shall *we* bring water for you out of this rock?" Israel has placed Moses at the center of this drama, and fatally he accepts that role. He has just proclaimed Aaron and himself to be saviors, failing to mention God as the real power. God's response is quick:

> And the LORD said to Moses and Aaron, "Because you did not believe in me, to uphold me as holy in the eyes of the people of Israel, therefore you shall not bring this assembly into the land that I have given them" (Num. 20:12).

The place was thereafter known as "Meribah," ('quarrelling' in Hebrew). This chapter ends with the death of Aaron, "because you rebelled against my command at the waters of Meribah" (Num. 20:24).

In addition, Moses will not be allowed to enter the promised land "because you broke faith with me in the midst of the people of Israel at the waters of Meribah-kadesh, in the wilderness of Zin, and because you did not treat me as holy in the midst of the people of Israel" (Deut. 32:51; Num. 27:14).

Spring Up Oh Well

Pulling up stakes in the wilderness south of the promised land, the children of Israel proceed to skirt around the land of Edom. Once again, the voices of complaint arise at the lack of food and water, as well as boredom with the manna that God has been providing (Num. 21:5). As a result, they are plagued with "fiery serpents." After several deaths, the people repent, apparently on their own this time, and come to Moses asking for intercession with the Lord. God tells Moses to create a fiery serpent and place it on a pole. Moses makes a bronze serpent and mounts it on a pole. If those who were bitten looked upon the bronze serpent they lived, hence the medical symbol of a serpent (or two) on a pole to this day.

What is useful to notice here is that despite continued complaints and issues, the cooperation between the people and Moses seems to have finally become regular and fixed. The rebellions have come to an end. Something else has happened as a result of this. Moses seems to have become comfortable in his leadership role.

114.   Moses and the Yoke of Fire

As Israel is skirting the land of Moab, the Lord has Moses gather the people so that He could provide water for them. Unlike earlier situations, this gathering seems jubilant. The elders gather to select a spot and a well is dug as a song is sung:

> "Spring up, O well!—Sing to it!—the well
> that the princes made, that the nobles of the
> people dug, with the scepter and with their
> staffs" (Num 21:17-18).

The sense is that of a jubilant confidence that God will work to provide the necessary water for the congregation and for all of their flocks.

When Israel comes to the doorstep of the promised land, they begin to cozy up to the Midianites who have fallen into the worship of Baal. As always, Israel's blatant dismissal of the God that has brought them out of Egypt and led them through the wilderness angers the Lord. Moses must order the judges of Israel, "Each of you kill those of his men who have yoked themselves to Baal of Peor" (Num. 25:5). A plague has begun once again.

In this case, Phinehas, grandson of Aaron, and thus a priest, chases down a chief of the Simeonites, who has married the daughter of one of the five kings of Midian. He kills both of them.

> And the LORD said to Moses, "Phinehas
> the son of Eleazar, son of Aaron the priest,
> has turned back my wrath from the people
> of Israel, in that he was jealous with my
> jealousy among them, so that I did not con-
> sume the people of Israel in my jealousy.

> Therefore say, 'Behold, I give to him my covenant of peace, and it shall be to him and to his descendants after him the covenant of a perpetual priesthood, because he was jealous for his God and made atonement for the people of Israel'" (Num. 25:10-13).

Another generation has stepped into the priesthood. In his zeal, Phinehas has shown that there will be leadership among the priesthood for the people of God as they enter the land of promise.

In Sight of the Promise

Moses knows that his time is short. It is not a surprise when God comes to him:

> "Go up into this mountain of Abarim and see the land that I have given to the people of Israel. When you have seen it, you also shall be gathered to your people, as your brother Aaron was, because you rebelled against my word in the wilderness of Zin when the congregation quarreled, failing to uphold me as holy at the waters before their eyes" (Num. 27:12-14).

Moses' one request is that a suitable successor be appointed to lead Israel. And so, Joshua, Moses' faithful assistant, is publicly commissioned before Israel to become the one to lead the children into the promised land (Num. 27:23).

> So Moses the servant of the LORD died there in the land of Moab, according to the word of the LORD, and he buried him in

the valley in the land of Moab opposite Beth-peor; but no one knows the place of his burial to this day. Moses was 120 years old when he died. His eye was undimmed, and his vigor unabated (Deu 34:5-7).

Discussion Points:

1. Moses had seemed to have overcome his anger, but suddenly stumbles in this regard. Why?

2. In your own words, why is God so upset with Moses and Aaron when they fail to honor God at the waters of Rephidim?

3. After Rephidim, it seems that Moses' leadership is finally accepted without reservation. Discuss how this may have affected the life of this band of wanderers.

4. Moses dies in sight of the promised land and so he has hope for his legacy as he gazes at the rolling hills across from him. Is it perhaps fitting that he dies with that hope rather than shouldering the problems of leadership in the new land?

Application:

1. As we have seen, Moses struggles with self-right-
    eous anger. Are there certain traits, possibly fam-
    ily traits, that cause you to do as God would have
    you do, or not do?

2. Are there times when you have failed to honor
    God as He should have been honored? Moses con-
    tinued to serve well, if not better, after admonish-
    ment. Can you do the same?

3. Think of situations in which you have had to work
    under someone that you didn't think was qualified
    to lead. Have you then changed your opinion?
    How did that change the atmosphere?

4. Hope is one the most profound virtues of Christi-
    anity. In a sense, we all face a promise that is 'over
    there,' just out of reach. Discuss how faith, hope
    and love color your personal disposition.

About the author:

William W. Wells is currently retired and writing, after a career as theatrical designer and a drafter. He studied for a Masters of Religious Education during an early period in a post-Christian religious cult. That occurred fifty years in the past, but for those interested to know more about those experiences see: *A Cult Challenge to the Church*, by the author. He is actively involved in a well centered charismatic church.

Wells is concerned to increase spiritual literacy in the church, by exploring spiritual giftings, but always with a respect for scripture and for the history and traditions of the church as a whole. Christ will return to one Body of Christ.

The author's other books include: *Job's White Funeral; Religion and God in the Bible's Most Confounding Book*, presenting a comprehensive look at the book of Job, and *David in the Wilderness*, a study of David's formative years before becoming king of Israel.

Find his books at: Amazon.com under "Wm W Wells."

www.ingramcontent.com/pod-product-compliance
Lightning Source LLC
Chambersburg PA
CBHW050734260726
48661CB00001B/221